Praise for *Empty Me Full*

"*Empty Me Full* is an invitation to intimate conversation with a wise and affectionate seeker. But Catherine Abbey Hodges is no common questioner. Hers is a wit-laced and vulnerable wondering as she looks back over a life—loss of parents and recollection of girlhood pleasures, long marriage and motherhood. Exhilarated by relationship with human, animal, earth and sky, in language honed with care and cadence, her surprising turns of thought and discovery deepen our shared humanity. Without being sentimental, the book is rich with sentiment. Without dictating belief, the collection inspires reverence for the greater-than-human. In poems that turn grief to awe and sadness to wonder, the poet celebrates our stunning, imperfect lives. When she allows, 'It's not a sad thing, / perhaps, to be always a bit sad' we sigh into our shared frailty. And when she encourages 'a nod, a long gaze, three deep bows,' we comply."

—Barbara Rockman
Author of *to cleave*

"'I sing of times trans-shifting,' said Robert Herrick, and so does Catherine Abbey Hodges in her new collection, *Empty Me Full*. She mingles elegies of loss with skillful praise of tenuous beauties in ways that make the heart rejoice even as it keeps on aching. These are gorgeous and thoughtful poems, self-consistent but full of surprising meanders and turns. Of all the poets that I know, Hodges is one of the few I return to again and again for repose and nourishment. 'Maybe time dreams us,' she says. 'Maybe it's alright to rest.'"

—Paul J. Willis
Author of *Somewhere to Follow*

"The poems in Catherine Abbey Hodges' *Empty Me Full* ask deep and necessary questions of both the speaker and her readers. How to define clarity? What is sorrow, and why must we accept it? Who best explains faith? And even, 'Does it matter?' But everything matters to this poet, and she hungers for a response, if not an easy resolution; 'Spendthrift / world, it's me again, listening hard,' she writes. This beautifully paced book is a lovely, inviting incantation to notice, to be aware, to live this world 'a little more awake,' and to always query, 'how did we / get here? And can we stay forever?'"

—Jen Karetnick
Author of *Inheritance with a High Error Rate*

"*In Empty Me Full*, Catherine Abbey Hodges tenderly interrogates the workings of time. She travels with remarkable ease through the liminal corridors between life and death, how we remember, and what we can know. 'What else don't we know?' asks the book's first poem. The answer: 'Almost / everything.' Her poetry carries in it a stillness that takes you into a brief respite of calm. Even death seems calm—recent death of her mother, a visitation from her dead father, the death of the stars. 'Because the end hovers,' she writes, 'I think we should kiss // and kiss and kiss....'"

—Donna Spruijt-Metz
Author of *General Release from the Beginning of the World*

EMPTY ME FULL

POEMS

CATHERINE ABBEY HODGES

GUNPOWDER PRESS • SANTA BARBARA
2024

Published by Gunpowder Press
David Starkey, Editor
PO Box 60035
Santa Barbara, CA 93160-0035

Front cover image: Caroline Allen, "San Antonio Creek, Ojai"

ISBN-13: 978-1-957062-18-1

Library of Congress Control Number: 2024918778

www.gunpowderpress.com

Gunpowder Press books are published by Gunpowder Poetry, a 501(c)(3) nonprofit literary organization based in Santa Barbara, California.

For Rob

CONTENTS

I

II

III

But poems are like dreams: in them you put what you don't know you know.

—Adrienne Rich

I

How It Goes

The river rose, rose some more,
and we learned *floodplain*.

As in: thank the fates there is one,
though we hadn't known it.

Thank all the stars above, those
that have gone out

and the ones still casting light
into a future we won't see.

What else don't we know? Almost
everything.

In time lapse images of the night sky,
the paths of the stars leave lit scars

on the torso of heaven. O let time
lapse. Then what?

The mice nesting in the piano—
the one bound for ruin in a meadow

under the arch of a dying oak
east of somewhere briefly famous—

let them dance on the strings,
make a new song.

Let the worm in the oak
dream as it chews.

Maybe Time Dreams Us

A small green spider, fancy
in her gold freckles, has cast
a line from one shore to the other
of my coffee cup while I've been
sitting on this rock, and I see I've lost
an hour or so of time—
                            which is what,
really? A set of web-slender hyphens
winking between what just happened
and what's coming next? Between
flickering scenes and gnawed pencils?
Or is time a seed, barbed, catching
rides on the world's children: bobcat,
field mouse, wren, old dog?
                            That dog's
gone missing, and the boy who loves
her calls and calls, at last sleeps
and dreams of a turquoise river,
a door in a rock. When he wakes
he lies quiet, remembering, slowly,
his life. He swings his feet to the cool
boards, calls again.
                            Maybe time is
the sound his mouth forms. Or time
is the dog, trotting far off, keeping
to shaded gullies now the sun's high,
dreaming of the boy. Maybe time
dreams us. Maybe it's alright to rest.

Falling Song

I allow myself eddies of meaning ...
in the overall wandering of mirroring mind:
but Overall is beyond me ... .
          —A. R. Ammons

Per the latest thinking, they're both right,
the gradualists and the catastrophists,
about how the Grand Canyon formed
and continues to form. All I know is that there
in the Canyon, I fell into my own interior. Now
I'm paying closer attention than usual, taking
it all personally. The mechanics of debris flow,
for instance. The histories of Zoroaster Granite,
Vishnu Schist, Bright Angel Shale—names I roll
in my mouth like lozenges from another world.
And how did the Canyon Wren find its way here?
Into my ribcage, I mean. Listen. There it is,
slot-canyon clear, that falling song. *Fill me*
empty, it goes. Then it goes *empty me full*.

Child at Sixty

Today I miss my mother,
three years gone.
It's a version of homesickness,
compounded now by a further loss:
the hot tang of the original sorrow
has cooled, and I find myself
bereft of that too, child at the window,
bewildered, fitful.

Yes, I've heard that absence can grow
into its own kind of presence.
But for now, my mother is missing
and I miss her. It's still mine
to miss her. Time, keep
your hands off what's mine.

The Tenderness of Rowboats

Six or seven overturned
spooning on the dock
lines and cleats at ease
loose knots breathing
the sea breathing
and blues
all the blues
blues and shifting light

Water laps
the dock
blues lap the light
light swallows
time

My mother in a tree
eight summers in
has not yet been raped

My dad in overalls
no shirt
barefoot on the porch
says a careless goodbye
to his mother
for the last time
(neither knows
this) as she bends
to kiss him

Solstice on the Middle Fork

First day
of my second summer
mother-

less. Unmother-
ed. How to say this? How

to be it?
It's not a metaphor,
this ache.

My neck and shoulders,
rib cage,

thighs. Ache.
Each sun-struck rock along
this bank

delivered by the river
and not gently.

As if the Trees

Consider the way bark
grows over the ragged tear
where a blue oak lost
a limb in a violent storm,
so that at length
the fiercest rip is rounded
in a kind of kindness.

Think of the way wind
and river polish rock,
how they buff and burnish.

The rough places
will be made smooth
proclaimed the prophet Isaiah.

It's as if the trees, as if
water and weather, heard.
As if they knew their worth,
and in their long ways
made it so, make it so.

Names across Water

The moon, waxing crescent, rose
in my circle of tea as I sat on the deck
in the last of the dark. Little skiff, coracle, balsa
canoe. Shifting myth of us, at harbor in a cup.
Now the sky's all color and light, neon contrails,
moon paling and home in her high meadow.
Across the river, a fox's wild cry, more raven
croak than dog bark.

                    Wherever else we are, love,
we're also in this silvery myth, chill waters below
and slapping the sides as we make the moves, large
and small, that keep our craft afloat. We edge
toward or away from the center. With our oars
or feet, we push off the sudden rock, the snag along
the bank. When we capsize, so far we've
surfaced gasping, called each other's names
across the water, found whatever floats.

On Moving toward Clarity

Broth? Which broth? The clear one,
or the one with egg and herbs?
Letter? Which one? First letter of your name?
Letter bearing news of a murder
or a prize? Letter of the law?
And station—which station is that?
The one by the sea, where you fed your sandwich to gulls
before your sister lifted you onto the train?
Or the station where Jesus fell for the third time
or the one where Veronica wiped his face?

Soon someone says *This is exhausting. There must*
be a flowchart, an app. Don't we have
a Ministry of Disambiguation?
It's a voice you know. Never mind.

Extreme clarity is a mystery,
wrote Darwish. We move toward it
by moving through possibilities with our bodies
and minds, our memories and dreams, as through a field
of heavy-headed grasses.
It helps to be hungry. It's helps to go alone.
It helps that sometimes, as evening comes, you'll see
a lit window on the field's far side, a door. Then you'll turn
the handle, step inside to find familiar, mysterious
faces, bread, perfectly clear
broth, steaming.

Here in this Wave

Where is he now,
the boy who said he could photosynthesize,
swore it was so from the third row
of tenth grade biology?
All these years, maybe I've hoped it could be true.
Maybe I've been running
experiments. This could explain
a few things, like the way,
when I stand under sunlight filtered
through sycamore leaves
or sieved through the lace of acacias, when I dream
myself into a kelp forest radiance, I feel
a fulness, nearly audible:
an orchestra tuning
here in the curl of a slow wave of light.

Ars Poetica with Jellyfish

Summer has almost poured itself out, but June's
moon jellyfish still swim, propel themselves
by expansion and contraction, rest and effort,
through my dreams.
                          They're all but invisible
under sunlight, these jellyfish, small windows
with old panes of wavy glass. What I see as a body
is known as a bell.

I Can't Place You, Flower

in that butane
blouse, and I won't be leafing
through a field guide for your ID—
it's immaterial like so much else I thought
I ought to know, each of us
immaterial at last,
and, say the physicists, always.
So much for the way of the flesh and the joy of more stuff.
Something in me always knew it was a hoax,
a lame joke. Still, what is this ache to touch
the combustible hem of your blue?
Why am I holding out
my disappearing
hand?

Having Now

Hoping for a fox
I almost miss the owl
  coming in low
    from across the river

  rustling like my life
  like a thought
I've almost had all this time
  and am having now.

II

Poem with Rilke and Two Dead Dogs

We were with new friends, the night had gone late,
      and the talk swung around to dogs we'd loved

and buried. I spoke of Lily, how we'd walked to the river
      and she'd frisked on her rickety hips one April evening,

how I'd found her dead the next morning. About my
      disbelief, even in a long season of losses during which

the tears hadn't come and hadn't come, not even when my mother
      had died two weeks earlier, and how Lily's body opened

that door. (How much of this I actually said I don't know.
      And does it matter?) Then Jim said that years ago,

when his boys were small, he too had awakened to find
      the life gone out of their family dog. He'd scooped

the dear old body up in his arms (a move less graceful
      and cinematic than it sounds, as you'll know

if you've done it) and put it in the back of his truck, obeying
      his first impulse to spare the children and take care

of arrangements once they were at school. But a truer,
      harder instinct followed, and he lifted the dog out

again so the boys would be able say their farewells. We're drawn
      to the easy thing, wrote Rilke to the young poet, but we

must hold ourselves to the difficult. Jim set himself up
      for the sorrow of his boys' sorrow, an early entry

in the long book of losses, his action as good as a letter.
Better. Once I had a friend who told me *When*

I start to love someone, I start teaching myself how to say
goodbye. And I thought *Who hurt you?* and *Get some help*

for that and, briefly, *Let me help you.* Thirty years later,
the list of things I don't understand longer all the time,

I understand he was more right than not. Also this:
that what we need from each other is more

than protection from the pain of endings.
What love requires is larger and more difficult

by far, a thing of substance, the big old dog
of truth, smelling of river and something further

afield, to companion us through the dark, press against
our legs. *Here is this terrible thing, this gone friend*

who yesterday was licking our faces and shedding
all over the couch. No, I can't stop death, my dears.

These tears wetting our cheeks? We'll splash him
with them, sing a little, tell each other stories.

Maybe we'll take the day off school. I'm telling you,
that's what I heard. Did Jim say it? To his boys?

To us that night? I don't know, and it doesn't
matter. But I think he said the bit about school.

Letter to Muriel

—in memory of John Ridland

One grey day you served us tangerine-carrot soup
for lunch. Was that before or after you put up a notice
for guests: *Bird nesting above front door, please come
around back*? Before the two of you left for Hungary,

you duct-taped foam to the sharp corners of counters
you'd judged to be the height of our son's forehead.
This was after you'd convinced us we'd be doing you
a favor by staying in your home while you were gone.

We were between rentals, impossibly young. On your
new patio of old stone, before the children woke,
before I drove into town to teach the one class
Santa Barbara City College had for me, I tried

to write poems—something you and John thought
I could do. A couple of them worked out, most didn't.
Some things don't change much. You'd left instructions
that included *We don't kill spiders—if they bother*

you, please take them outside. Later, once you'd returned
and we'd moved far inland, you wrote us about a visitor—
a small fox. How for weeks you saw it in the afternoon,
under the oaks in the filtered sunlight, curled

nose-to-tail in the shallow basin of a boulder. I knew
the place, the warmth of the sandstone, the even pulse
of trust. All this was long ago, of course. I still taste
that bright soup, though, and I know how that fox felt.

I hope I wrote you back. If I didn't, here's the tardy letter.
And if I did, here it is again from further on—thanking
you, bereft with you, remembering with love.

Message to My Daughter on the Birth of Her First Child

Meet your new teacher, little Buddha, baby Jesus,
eight pounds and counting of hunger and wonder.

On the way to becoming herself, she'll do her job,
school you, like her mother did her mother.

Try to get some rest now. Try not to think so hard.
From here on out it's mostly paradox.

First Marriage

When I was a child I ran off
      with a morning of rain. No one
            approved, but what did we care?
                It was love.

We made plans,
      spoke of secret rivers,
            my lost dragonfly,
                the kingdom of grasses.

We lived together
      wild and content,
            our quarrels brief,
                forever,

                        made for each other,
            until mid-afternoon.

Sisters in the Fog

The swallows in their joy dives through the rising
dusk haven't heard your diagnosis. I wish

I could hate or at least resent them, but all
I can muster is envy—that and an ache I can taste

for those mornings we shivered in our Speedos
on the starting blocks, small wood ducks ready to fall

into our lives, our toes curled over the edge, the chlorine-
scented fog so thick we could hardly see each other

as we waited to drop into the blue
that we took on faith stretched all the way to the far end.

A Room that Moves as You Move

—*after Seamus Heaney*

You slip into a meaning made of river.
No, be precise: of snowmelt, raindrops, clouds,
of tea-brown streams from deep inside the hills.
From peaky mountains, bright mineral runnels.

These bid welcome to your body, make a space,
a room that moves as you move, and moves you
with the current, sensation before thought.
You travel on through deconstructed sky.

All Day the Stars

—after W. S. Merwin

You told me when you're gone
      you will be rain.
Look for Cygnus
      in the ditch you said.
All day the stars
      an alphabet of light
chant in the hall
      spell the one thing.
Days ride the air
      on their way away forever.
See how the stars look back
      as if they weren't in love with death.
See how the stars look back
      on their way away forever.
Days ride the air
      chant an alphabet of light
spell the one thing
      in the next room.
All day the stars
      swim hidden in the ditch
and still no Cygnus
      though you will be rain
you said. And here you are.

On Seeing the SpaceX Satellite Train
from the Floor of the Grand Canyon

Bruce had put away his glasses
and said he saw a bar of light. Someone else
saw a chain of neon hyphens. I flashed
back decades to a nighttime train,
lit windows like comic strip panes
passing too fast and far away to read.

Later, the spectacle over, it was a comfort
to be alone again with constellations
we'd known all our lives and further-off
smudges and smears of light—
our feeble acquaintance
with infinity—never mind
that those lights too had moved on,
each on its own inscrutable rails.

Autumn Again

One afternoon, I pretended
to be a cat—tabby, kinked tail.
And the finches behaved
accordingly. Then September

flew past with its pears
and empties. Speaking of empty,
the sky, but only till my eyes
adjust. October? You

love it for old time's sake,
as do I you. Again you choose it
from the drop-down menu.
Now here's our mother, back

from the attic, back from the dead,
lugging the box of costumes.

Places to Look after You've Looked Everywhere Else

Ahead of the day's first drink and ceremony
of intentions; ahead of the ringing
from two doors down, ahead of the fields
of blue and crates of weather-pulped
magazines; ahead of the last horse; ahead of skies
like lake beds; ahead of lakes.

Behind the shoulder of the island and badly reset
arm; behind the curtain and pane,
the spangle of dust; behind the vellum lamp shade,
behind the music stand; behind the after
and rattle of trees; behind the times
that almost delivered.

Ahead of the reverse jackknife from lake to cloud;
behind the threadbare sky. Ahead of the train,
squint-bright in late sun, the shuddered
tracks; behind the back door, banging.
Ahead of the ribbon-cutting in the wind.
Behind every last mirror in the hall.

I'll Speak in Code for as Long as It Takes

A girl sits at a piano for three generations,
        hands above the keys just so.
Dressed as a sparrow, a ghost
        taps at the pane.
Now September's tossed coin
        goes missing among the hills.
To the east of these words
        a mouse builds a nest of frayed ribbon.
Here's where you hold your breath
        and start to count
as night swells with the absence
        of Palestrina.
Trust me, says the ghost. *In the fullness of time*
        you'll make your best mistakes.

There must be someone to thank

was how my mother explained
the beginning of her belief in God.
The way she told it, half my life ago,
the thought took her by surprise
and was thereafter utterly convincing,
as real and workaday as the wicker
mending basket that sat at the end
of the hall. Now I'm looking into
a beige-gone-turquoise sky, struck
by how little I know on the subject
of what can and can't be mended,
thinking of my parents and siblings,
of sunburns, the smoke from birthday
candles, other shreds of childhood.
For a moment it's as if I'm looking up
through water, my eyes stinging a little
and everything strangely lit and shifting.
Geese change places in their skein overhead.
A snatch of song I used to know flares
from the window of a passing car. I look
around for someone to thank, someone
to remind me the name of that song.

Old Blue Shirt

A time zone away, someone I love
is taking a test. For him, I've tried
to hold myself still for a square inch
of time. It's the least I can do
and the most, something like prayer,
but less wordy. This is the boy who saw
an angel down a dim hallway at dawn.
Years later, another in the Grand
Canyon: mineral visitor, feathered flood
and flame. Something passed between
them, I think, though I didn't want to pry.
I haven't seen an angel, but I've taken
years of tests, lately of my vision,
my platelets, my capacity for stillness.
Oh wait a minute. Could the bird
that sang *sweetie sweetie sweetie*
a moment ago really be singing *stupid*
stupid stupid now to the same tune?
In my mind a table. On it, the usual
mess, sweet and stupid, stupid and sweet,
and me in my old blue shirt, in a chair
from a long-gone kitchen, looking
out the window at myself looking in,
and both of us thinking: how did we
get here? And can we stay forever?

Hearing from My Dad

Watering the basil,
I disturb a hundred bees,
whereupon every bee poem
I've ever read sets up a hum

in my chest, and now
the sky's turned strange
as well, a kind of abalone light,
which makes me wonder

if I may be having an ecstatic
experience of modest proportions.
      Would you look at that
says my dad, from the other side

of time, interested as always.
He could mean the tangled herbs.
He could mean me, this new
translucence, wing of a bee.

Bloom and Bloom

Here I'd assumed one poem about jacaranda blossoms
underfoot would be my lifetime quota. But that misses
the point, since I know I won't know till I'm well in

or done what the thing is *about*, that filament, shred
                       of incandescence, essence

to which, if anything can get close, it will be a poem feeling its way,
              talking to itself between silences.

I'm here for that, or in the next room, ear to the wall. Spendthrift
               world, it's me again, listening hard,

talking you up, extolling your gullies and beetles, your bruised
blossoms on the pavement, the ones that bloom
and bloom even once they're dust.

That Bell in Your Hand

After weeks of brilliant sun, Delft skies,
petals in the air, petals in the gutters,
today dawned grey. Sudden gusts

of wind knocked pollen from the pines.
Then I heard the voice in me that's silent
except in times of great sorrow

or great excitement say
Bring it Bring it Bring it! So I dug
through the closet and found the bells,

handed one to everyone I've ever loved.
That's why you have that bell in your hand.
It's why we're out here dancing with the dead.

Been and Gone

How many times—hundreds, thousands—did Dad
lift Mom's glasses from her face with his slim fingers,
take them to the sink, run them under cool water, rub
each lens between his thumb and index finger with a dab
of soap, then rinse, then dry them on a tea towel.

He'd set them back on her nose, slip the wires behind
her ears with elaborate care, and she'd laugh: how fresh
it all looked, her life! The wall clock, the recipe, the knobs
on the stove. Dust motes in late sun. Smudge and glimmer,
life that's been and gone, and me here telling.

III

Williwaw

Something spools from the foamy
elderberry blossoms. The world is wordy.

I've made peace with that, as long as nobody
says anything most of the time. But today

I'm hearing *williwaw williwaw* in my own
voice. Augusts ago we spent a night at a rainy

campground by that name, which my mouth
loved saying even more than I loved

its meaning: a wind that sweeps down
off a mountain range over coastal waters.

A dim memory: saying *milk milk milk* aloud
to myself so many times that I finally felt

the word's meaning fall away. Then *milk*
became only a sound spilling from the small

cave in my face as my lips opened, the sound
changing as the tip of my tongue met the roof

of my mouth just behind my front teeth,
changing again as the back of my tongue

rose and made a little plosive before
my lips closed and I started over. So many

years later—so much striving, the seas
of meaning and meaninglessness

in which I've thrashed about—what if all I want
now is to say *williwaw* again and again until

I'm back in that tent wiping raindrops from your
face. Thence, per the pattern, back to sound

as sound, elderberry blossoms as themselves,
the short trip from there back to silence.

Story Ending in a Heap of Boards

Next door, an old shed's coming down.
The neighbor sent a text yesterday,
said they'd be starting early.

Arced spine of persimmon leaf,
simmer where field meets sky, the way
river flows around rock. Some days

almost everything's about sex, and maybe
this as well: groan of old boards, joists
and beams remembering, music

of breaking glass. It's taking a long time.
It sounds as if they're being delicate
about it. That shed went up forty years ago,

fifty, back when silences crashed louder
than sunlight. Hush of bark curling,
leaves unfurling. By now, fingers

of afternoon light through the oaks
will be soothing the splintered wood,
spangling shards of windowpane.

I feel you, heap of bones and light.
This, too, I'm claiming for Eros.

There's a Day

There's a day you want back—
not to change anything,
just to live it a little more awake.
But of course that would change it.

Outfielder

Now that this day's returned
to mind, the scrappy team
in the burning-off fog,
everyone a little buzzed
on everyone else
and the smells of a late-
April-early-May beach town,
the memory plays
in reverse:

first the jolt, almost electric,
then the ball sucked back out
of the mitt, spitting sparks
like a miniature comet, the girl
running beneath it as it arced back
toward the stars behind the day-lit sky
then down again to the pop of impact,
the rewound swing, the pitch
returned to sender

while the outfielder
who'd make that future catch
wondered what sex
would feel like and whether Jesus
could come back as a blade of grass
and if the last shreds of fog
were in her chest
or in the branches
of the trees.

Leftover Sonnet

On the slope below my window, a man
in a blue t-shirt and grass-stained jeans
is pulling weeds. Oh! It's the one I married,

the boy with the curly hair and sweet voice,
a few decades on. October afternoon, warm
breeze. At breakfast we'd agreed to reheat

last night's curry for dinner, leftovers
having emerged as something of a theme for us.
As in: what's left of us, now the kids are gone.

As in: suppose we take what's left and kick
it up a notch, now the flavors have settled in.
As if he's heard my thoughts, he looks up at me,

grins, waves a fistful of filaree my direction
before he tucks and rolls down the hill.

Another Kind of Light

At last and all of a sudden,
here it is: the afternoon to turn
summer's last tomatoes—
some on the sill, others still
on the vine—into soup to freeze
for the cold to come.

You take the chipped yellow
bowl from the high shelf
and we head to the garden.
Overhead, what someone
called a buttermilk sky, sky
banking left from the long
bright days toward winter,
which is to say a mortal sky,
sky-sign of endings, death-
facing sky, still burnished
with summer's last syllables.
We fill the bowl again
and again with tomatoes
warm and heavy in their skins.

Later, we'll listen
to what we can bear of the news,
and I'll refuse the violence
that won't end and must end
a place at the table
of this one poem
while the tomatoes burble
in their complex juices,

fragrant with the further
complications, complicities
if you will, of garlic
and rosemary.

We'll look at each other.
It's too much, you'll say,
or I will—we take turns
as we used to tell the children
to do, and I lose track. Maybe
we'll step outside where the early
stars will argue for the hundredth
time that the dark overtaking
the sky is another kind of light.
Though we'll shake our heads
as always, maybe this time
we'll pray that somehow
they know something
we don't.

By Which I Mean Repent

At my feet, on a plant we call
a weed, the star-shaped husks
of five small flowers form
a new constellation, named
by nobody. Oh friends,

what if we dropped to our knees
before what's hidden, overlooked?
Acacia pods, for instance. Pebbles
on their long, specific ways
toward sand. Ants about their

herculean errands. What if we
praised all that has escaped
our naming, composed hymns
to the limits of our sovereignty,
gathered to sing them? We could

listen to the tongues of the small
of the earth, revise our ways,
by which I mean, you understand,
repent. We could. That sound
like dry leaves lifted by a breeze,

then set down rearranged? I'm
thinking: what if that sound
is salvation rustling in the field
where our dominion ends
and everything else begins.

To a Mountain Garter Snake

There you were again, slipping away so imperceptibly
I wouldn't have seen you had I not been on the alert.

After four sightings in a week of your sleek darkness
and lightning stripes, the silent parting of grasses

as you whipped away under arches heavy with seed heads,
I'd come to think of you as a tacit friend. Today, though,

when I stopped short to admire your swift passage, you too
stopped, then raised your severe head on your slender

neck, which is also your body, above the litter of winter's
sycamore leaves and spring's tangle of vetch, and I heard

myself gasp. For a minute or so, we regarded each other,
both of us motionless. Some time into this arrangement,

I thought something like *Now we're getting somewhere,
we've crossed a threshold*, and was happy and awestruck

and grateful. But as I kept my gaze on you in your ascendance
above the tan leaves, the green net of vetch and the purple

blossoms like tiny bells, I knew I'd mistaken the threshold,
that I knew next to nothing, and you not at all. That you're

a mystery familiarity won't solve, only deepen. And after
you returned to your errand, your realm, I stood there long

in the changing light, happy and awestruck and grateful.

None of Us Were Dying Then

—for Staff Sgt. Donald Shue and my mother, in memoriam

You were reading *The Inner Game
of Tennis*. Nixon was looking
straight into the camera.
POW/MIA bracelets
were trending,
and I was polishing
finger-prints off mine with the hem
of one peasant blouse
or another.
        That summer we moved
to the house you would die in
45 years later, though none
of us were dying or would ever
die then, and the older girl
next door was shipped
to Canada on account
of her drug habit
to be reborn a fable
like the burned-out
Bank of America
in Isla Vista.
        It was a time of surfaces
and things that won't come back, though
I'm back now with questions I didn't ask
then. *How was the book, Mom?* and *Do
you know where I put that bracelet?*
All these wars later, I can't
even remember
taking it off.

After the Flood

They looked like goners,
the cottonwoods and alders
downed when the river
went wild. And no wonder:
for two days we'd heard
the boom of boulders
above the water's roar,
heard the crash and snap
of sturdy trees.

But now they're sprouting
branches, new green
thrusting skyward
from prone trunks.

It's a strange sight, hopeful
though not yet beautiful,
this ungainly resurrection,
early days of a miracle
etched in the seed.

Now It Occurs to Me

that I will always, from here
on out, be a little melancholy.
That in fact this is nothing
new. Since childhood, mine
what we call a happy one
notwithstanding, my face
in repose an old airfield
in the rain. It's not a sad thing,
perhaps, to be always a bit sad.
It's a nod to what has earned,
will earn, the sadness, to so much
of what we call *this life*. A nod,
a long gaze, three deep bows.

River of Stars over the Grand Canyon

Now that the moon has slipped
behind the canyon walls,
the river of stars between the high rims
      cools the granites and shales

as we lie awake together and alone
with our wordless questions,
the Colorado speaking in tongues close by.
      To think it might be offering answers—

well, that's some worrisome hubris.
Maybe the river's raising
questions of its own or praising the net
      of starlight that spangles its surface.

Does it matter? It's enough
just to be here. Years from now, in far-distant
beds, we'll wake in the night
      and say it again: it's enough.

In the Event that You Find This

Try to remember the moon
        itself is never less than full.
                The evening cashier has a secret

sorrow and plans for the weekend.
        Each spoon its history, each stone.
                Recall, too, how the shoreline now

isn't last night's shore
        and not tomorrow's. And try
                to remember you didn't foresee

us here three years ago
        or yesterday, didn't know
                we'd be meeting (neither did I)

in this chapel or kitchen or poem,
        and you—you the one to close
                the deal, make it so, bring it home.

Planning for the End

Because the end hovers
without landing, acting

like it doesn't see us here
although it must,

and the rising stars
are headed to the planetarium

for solace and popcorn,
I think we should kiss

and kiss and kiss and see
where that gets us.

Bird of Impossible Dimensions

... everything
is changed forever all the time.
—Bob Hicok

This afternoon some cirrus clouds
formed the wings of a huge bird
and it felt important that a bird of impossible
dimensions would be spreading its wings
over Central California. I like beauty
as much as the next person and those wings
were so beautiful I hurt my neck
trying to make out the rest of the bird but no luck
it had left its wings there
starting to fray a little
at the edges and come apart a little where they
joined and I thought maybe that was important too
along with the fact that they were still beautiful
as they were coming apart
as they became
something
else.

NOTES

The book's epigraph is from Adrienne Rich's essay "When We Dead Awaken: Writing as Re-Vision."

The epigraph to "Falling Song" is from "Corson's Inlet" by A. R. Ammons.

"Here in this Wave" is for Neal Abello, my high school biology teacher.

"Having Now" is for Mim Abbey, who knows why, and for Margo Wilson, who long ago loaned us an owl.

"Message to My Daughter on the Birth of Her First Child" is for Clara Hodges Zimmerman.

The first line of "A Room that Moves as You Move" is a nod of awe to Seamus Heaney's "Squarings," xxxi.

"Hearing from My Dad" is for Jim Wimmer and Peggy White. Long may their basil flourish.

"All Day the Stars" owes thanks to W. S. Merwin's "Rain Light."

The epigraph to "Bird of Impossible Dimensions" is from "Some things that come together in coming apart" by Bob Hicok.

Mac Hodges made the Grand Canyon poems possible, and they are for him.

ACKNOWLEDGMENTS

My thanks to the editors of the following publications, in which a number of the poems in this book first appeared or are forthcoming, some in earlier versions or under different titles:

The American Journal of Poetry: "On Seeing the Space-X Satellite Train from the Floor of the Grand Canyon," "Poem with Rilke and Two Dead Dogs"

Anacapa Review: "Leftover Sonnet," "Mountain Garter Snake," "There's a Day"

CALYX: A Journal of Art and Literature by Women: "Autumn Again," "In the Event that You Find This," "Story Ending in a Heap of Boards"

Crosswinds Poetry Journal: "Falling Song"

Gyroscope Review: "Bird of Impossible Dimensions," "By Which I Mean Repent"

I-70 Review: "I Can't Place You, Flower," "Maybe Time Dreams Us"

Narrative: "None of Us Were Dying Then"

Plume: "How It Goes," "Now It Occurs to Me"

Quire: A Literary Tract from the Last Press: "Places to Look after You've Looked Everywhere Else," "River of Stars over the Grand Canyon," "Sisters in the Fog," "That Bell in Your Hand," "There must be someone to thank"

Ruminate Magazine: "All Day the Stars"

SALT: "As if the Trees," "Letter to Muriel," "Old Blue Shirt," "On Moving toward Clarity," as well as reprints of "Places to Look after You've Looked Everywhere Else," "River of Stars over the Grand Canyon," "Sisters in the Fog," "That Bell in Your Hand," "*There must be someone to thank*"

SOLO Voyage: "Child at Sixty"

SWWIM: "Another Kind of Light"

Tar River Poetry: "Solstice on the Middle Fork"

Writing Fields: "Outfielder"

"Falling Song" was a finalist for the *Crosswinds Poetry Journal* Poetry Prize.

"All Day the Stars" was a finalist for the Janet McCabe Poetry Prize from *Ruminate Magazine*.

When I first saw "San Antonio Creek, Ojai," Caroline Allen's beautiful painting, I felt I'd already seen it in a dream. Her consent to its use for the book's cover is a tremendous gift.

For a shared residency with Rob Hodges, during which the manuscript that became this book reimagined itself, gratitude to the Helen Riaboff Whiteley Center at the University of Washington's Friday Harbor Labs.

For the gifts of time and solitude that created space for new poems and further refinement after I'd thought the manuscript finished (surprise!), my thanks to Peggy White and Jim Wimmer.

Further gratitude to Dean Diaz de Leon, Lise Goett, Rob Hodges, Lisa Gluskin Stonestreet and Paul Willis for suggestions that improved a number of the poems over the years of their writing; to Christopher Buckley for generous friendship and guidance; and to Peter Everwine and John Ridland in memoriam for their support and encouragement at just the right times.

Nourishing and wide-ranging conversations with Ann Marie Wagstaff and Lisa Crawford Lewis are in the DNA of several of the poems; I give thanks for and to these friends.

A deep bow to David Starkey and Chryss Yost of Gunpowder Press for all they do for poetry and poets, and for bringing *Empty Me Full* from manuscript to book.

Thanks always to my family of origin: Donna and Laurie Abbey in memoriam, and Russell, Anna, and Mim Abbey.

And to Rob, Clara, and Mac Hodges, my love and gratitude forever.

About the Poet

Catherine Abbey Hodges is the author of the poetry collections *Instead of Sadness*, selected by Dan Gerber for the 2015 Barry Spacks Poetry Prize from Gunpowder Press; *Raft of Days* (Gunpowder Press, 2017); and *In a Rind of Light* (Stephen F. Austin State University Press, 2020). Her chapbook *All the While* (Finishing Line Press, 2006) was a finalist in the New Women's Voices contest, and a letterpress chapbook, *A Spell for What Comes Next*, came out from Miramar Editions in 2018. Her poems appear widely in venues including *Plume, Narrative, The Southern Review, Tar River Poetry, CALYX, Miramar, Atticus Review, SALT, Chicago Quarterly Review, Cider Press Review, SWWIM, I-70 Review,* and *Gyroscope Review*. They've been anthologized, featured on *The Writer's Almanac* and *Verse Daily*, and nominated for the Pushcart Prize, the Orison Anthology, and Best of the Net. English Professor Emeritus at Porterville College and co-founder of Canyon Wren Writing Workshops, Catherine writes, edits, teaches privately, and collaborates with musician Rob Hodges on ancestral Yokuts land in the foothills of California's Sierra Nevada.

www.ingramcontent.com/pod-product-compliance
Lightning Source LLC
Chambersburg PA
CBHW031252120626
46545CB00007B/2778